Navigating Testing & Quality Assurance

Aliaksandr Khvastovich

(aka alexusadays)

Copyright © 2024 Aliaksandr Khvastovich

All rights reserved.

DISCLAIMER NOTICE

The information contained within this book is provided for educational and entertainment purposes only. All opinions expressed in this book are solely those of the author and do not represent the opinions or viewpoints of any organizations, companies, or institutions. By using the information provided in this book, you acknowledge that you do so voluntarily and accept full responsibility for your actions. The author and publisher are not responsible for any errors, omissions, or the results obtained from the use of this information.

Readers acknowledge that the author is not engaged in the rendering of any legal, financial, medical, or other professional advice. If professional advice or assistance is required, the services of a competent professional should be sought.

LIMITATION OF LIABILITY

By reading this book, you agree that the author and publisher are not liable for any damages or losses arising from the use or interpretation of the information contained within. This includes, but is not limited to, direct, indirect, incidental, punitive, and consequential damages. The author and publisher are not responsible for any actions taken based on the content of this book, and the information is used at your own risk.

Navigating Testing & Quality Assurance

DEDICATION

To my parents, my kids, and my wife Maryia, thank you for your unwavering support, love, and encouragement.

CONTENTS

CONTENTS

ABOUT THE AUTHOR 1
CHAPTER 1: THE BASIS OF TESTING...............................2
   WHAT IS TESTING? 4
   TESTING IN DIFFERENT INDUSTIES 6
   IMPORTANCE OF TESTING..8
CHAPTER 2: BECOMING A TESTER..................................10
   WHY BECOME A TESTER? 12
   THE FUTURE OF TESTING...14
   HOW TO BECOME A TESTER? 17
   CURRENT QA TRENDS...20
   BECOMING A GREAT TESTER 24
CHAPTER 3: SDLC AND METHODOLOGIES......................28
   INTRO TO THIS CHAPTER 30
   SDLC..31
   WATERFALL METHODOLOGY 33
   AGILE METHODOLOGY 35
   REALITY OF METHODOLOGIES....................................39
CHAPTER 4: TYPES OF TESTING 42
   DIFFERENT TYPES OF TESTING 44
CHAPTER 5: BUGS 48

    WHAT IS A BUG 50

    BUG LIFE CYCLE 54

CHAPTER 6: THE REALITY OF TESTING 60

    INTRO TO THIS CHAPTER 62

    AUTOMATE EVERYTHING 62

    LACK OF DOCUMENTATION 67

    DEV QA 71

    QA STRATEGY 78

CHAPTER 7: JOB SEARCH & CAREER GROWTH 86

    JOIN QA COMMUNITY 88

    LEARN TRENDING TOOLS 90

    STAY UP TO DATE 92

CONCLUSION 96

ACKNOWLEDGMENTS

To my friends and colleagues in the QA field, thank you for inspiring me with your dedication and expertise. Your passion for quality and continuous improvement has been a guiding force throughout my journey.

I would like to thank the QA community and my viewers, for being an essential part of my journey. Your engagement and enthusiasm continue to motivate me to learn and share more.

And a special thanks to ChatGPT for helping me with editing and ensuring this book is clear, polished, and readable.

ABOUT THE AUTHOR

Hi everyone, my name is Aliaksandr Khvastovich, but you might know me as alexusadays on YouTube. I am an immigrant from Belarus who came to the United States in 2008, and I have been passionately working in the field of Quality Assurance since 2012.

My career began with a bootcamp and freelance as a QA engineer on uTest. Since then, I have had the privilege of working as a QA engineer across multiple companies and industries, including Wi-Fi, eCommerce, Cryptocurrency, Web Based Gaming, Medical APIs, and Banking.

Over the years, I have taken on various roles in QA, including Manual QA engineer, Senior QA, Full-stack QA, QA manager, and QA automation engineer. These experiences have shaped my perspective and deepened my understanding of this exciting field.

At the time of working on this book, I also help as a QA instructor at Careerist, aspiring QA professionals start their careers and grow in the field.

In this book, I try to share some of my ideas about Quality Assurance, the lessons I have learned, and the insights I have gained. Here you might find some practical advice, testers' wisdom, and observations that I hope will resonate with you.

All my professional experience comes from working in the United States, so the content may feel especially relevant to those navigating a similar environment

CHAPTER 1: THE BASIS OF TESTING

Navigating Testing & Quality Assurance

WHAT IS TESTING?

If you picked up this book, chances are you are either curious about testing or already working in the field and looking for fresh perspectives.

As I see it, testing is more than just finding bugs, it is a process of improving product quality, ensuring compliance with requirements and regulations, and delivering a product that meets or exceeds user expectations.

Testing ensures that the products you work on can stand strong in a competitive market, offering a positive user experience by minimizing issues and maximizing reliability. Testing plays a pivotal role in shaping the success of any product.

In my personal experience, a tester serves as a crucial bridge between developers and business. Testers promote a mindset of quality the organization. They verify that products meet requirements, approach issues from the user's perspective, and proactively suggest improvements.

Quality Assurance (QA) professionals play a vital role in ensuring product quality and reliability.

QA key responsibilities include:

- Detecting and documenting issues to ensure their visibility.
- Creating test plans and scenarios based on business requirements.
- Executing detailed tests to verify functionality, usability, performance, etc.
- Providing actionable feedback and assessing potential risks.

TESTING IN DIFFERENT INDUSTIES

When working in Quality Assurance (QA) across various organizations and industries, it is important to understand that testing practices will differ significantly. Some industries may be more relaxed, relying on your expertise to establish and follow QA processes, while others may be highly regulated, adhering to strict standards and regulations.

For example, Industries like medical devices and aerospace require an elevated level of organizational, verification, and regulatory compliance. In these fields, testing must be rigorous and repeatable, with every step meticulously followed. There is zero tolerance for shortcuts, as lives and critical systems depend on absolute precision and reliability.

On the other hand, in fast-paced startups, development is driven by requirements set by business. Startups may prioritize speed and agility to stay competitive, which means requirements can change frequently and updates are often fast-tracked. As a tester, you will need to adapt to shifting priorities. This level of flexibility is much harder to achieve in well regulated industries, where strict processes and compliance standards are fundamental to development processes.

Company culture also plays a significant role. A culture that values Quality and open communication promotes better Quality Assurance processes and collaboration across different teams. In contrast, a culture that prioritizes speed over quality may require testers to navigate tighter deadlines and shift priorities to accommodate business.

It does not matter whether the industry is gaming, medical, or navigation software, Quality Assurance is essential. However, the processes, tools, and testing dynamics will vary based on industry standards, regulatory requirements, company size, and organizational culture.

IMPORTANCE OF TESTING

Would you fly on a plane that had not been tested? Of course not. Testing ensures the safety, reliability, and usability of products we rely on daily. Without proper quality assurance, navigation systems could fail, devices could crash, and games might not load.

Modern products are incredibly complex, with multiple layers of integration. Skipping testing is not an option, as it can halt progress, disrupt industries, and lead to costly failures. Without proper testing, serious issues can arise. A notable example would be the CrowdStrike outage, where a critical bug caused widespread disruptions. You can learn more by searching online for "CrowdStrike outage".

Proper testing ensures products are safe, functional, and user-friendly, while a lack of testing leaves users to discover issues themselves — a surefire way to damage trust and reputation. As a QA professional, you should understand the critical role testing plays in making products better.

Remember that end users are everyday people like you and me. In fact, I once found myself using a commercial version of an internet modem that had Wi-Fi chip I worked on. This experience made the importance of quality assurance even more personal.

To summarize, Quality Assurance is essential. Proper testing ensures that products work as intended, it prevents unexpected failures and creates positive user experiences. Proper QA processes and testing builds trust and confidence in products, apps, and devices we rely on every day.

CHAPTER 2: BECOMING A TESTER

Navigating Testing & Quality Assurance

WHY BECOME A TESTER?

Before we talk about how to become a tester, let us talk about why one should become a tester. Quality Assurance field offers job security, career growth, and competitive salaries. QA salaries are often not far behind those of software developers. But beyond financial incentives, there are several compelling reasons to pursue a career as a tester.

High demand and job security:
Every software product, app, or system must be tested before it reaches users. As technology evolves and companies race to release new features, the demand for QA testers only grows. QA professionals are needed in every industry that has code. Simply put, as long as the software exists, so will the need for skilled testers.

Lower barrier to entry:
Compared to development roles, QA is more accessible to people from non-technical backgrounds. You do not need a computer science degree to become a tester. A lot of people enter QA field through bootcamps, self-study, or freelance projects on platforms like uTest. This makes QA one of the most accessible entry points into tech.

Career development:
You can start as manual testers and move on to roles like QA Automation Engineer, QA Manager, SDET, or even QA Director. For those who enjoy coding, learning automation can significantly boost career growth and salary potential.

Remote work opportunities:
QA roles are among the most remote-friendly tech positions. Often companies offer fully remote or hybrid work options, allowing testers to maintain a flexible work-life balance. This is especially valuable for those seeking location independence.

Diverse work environment:
As a QA tester, you will have the opportunity to work across multiple industries, including healthcare, fintech, gaming, web development, and many other. Every product requires testing, and each industry comes with its own unique challenges, tools, and skills. This variety keeps the job fresh and engaging.

Continuous learning:
Testers are always learning, investigating, and problem-solving. If you enjoy critical thinking, analysis, and continuous improvement, QA will keep you engaged.

THE FUTURE OF TESTING

So, you are thinking about becoming a tester but keep hearing conflicting information about the state of the QA job market and the future of the field. Maybe You have also heard concerns about AI replacing developers and testers or that everything will be automated in the future, leaving no need to write or test code anymore. Let me share my perspective on this.

We live in a world surrounded by code. Millions of products are in development, with countless more hitting the market every day. Existing products are constantly competing for market share, which requires continuous updates and improvements. Take Instagram, for example. Before Facebook acquired it, it was a simple app for uploading photos with filters. Today, it is a platform for influencers, featuring short and long videos, a marketplace, video filters, ad placements, integrations with other services, and more.

Product improvement is an ongoing process. As long as a product is competing in the market, development never stops.
While some aspects of testing can be automated, automation is not a "set it and forget it" solution. Every time a product evolves, automation scripts

must be updated too. And what happens if there is a bug in the automation itself or even in the AI? Who will test the AI testers to ensure they are working properly? That is where human testers come in.

Additionally, certain types of testing simply cannot be automated, like testing wearable devices that monitor heart rate or oxygen levels. Highly regulated industries also require human oversight to meet strict compliance standards.

If you are concerned about the future of QA, consider this: search for "quality assurance US Bureau of Labor Statistics projected growth" and you will see that development and QA positions are projected to grow by 17% from 2023 to 2033 — faster than the average for most other occupations. The demand for QA professionals is not going anywhere.

Anything involving code and intended for public use needs to be tested. What many people do not realize is just how much code surrounds us. For instance, try to guess how many lines of code are in a modern car. Not a smart car like a Tesla — just a regular car. Got a guess? Maybe 10,000? 100,000?

The actual answer is around 150 million lines of

code. We are essentially driving computers without even realizing it. Code is everywhere — in your TV, toaster, coffee maker, phone, and countless other devices. As technology becomes increasingly complex and interconnected, the need for quality assurance will only grow.

In my opinion, the role of QA professionals is more critical than ever. **In a world dominated by code, testing serves as the backbone of innovation, safety, and user trust.**

HOW TO BECOME A TESTER?

So, how does one become a tester? Since there is no official university degree in Quality Assurance, how do people break into the field? Do they migrate from development roles, start with a computer science degree, or transition from other tech positions? The truth is, there are many paths to becoming a tester.

Unlike traditional careers with a clear academic path, QA offers flexibility in how you start. People enter through bootcamps, online courses, freelance testing platforms, or self-study.

For instance, if you search for my YouTube channel, "alexusadays," you will find a variety of Quality Assurance videos that can help guide you through this process. In the United States, a combination of bootcamp training, a strong resume, and solid interview skills can land you a QA job.

In other countries, certifications like ISTQB (International Software Testing Qualifications Board) are often a popular and sometimes required qualification for job placement. While this certification is not as essential in the U.S., it can be a useful addition to your resume, especially if you plan to apply for roles outside the United States.

If you're looking for the fastest, most effective way to break into the QA industry with zero experience, you can try and follow this path:

- **Freelance experience:**

Start by signing up for crowdsourced testing platforms like uTest or Testlio. This will give you hands-on experience testing real-world products.

- **QA bootcamp:**

Then enroll in a QA bootcamp where you'll learn the basics of manual testing, QA processes, and technical skills.

- **Certification:**

Then learn and obtain certification in a modern automation tool like Playwright, as automation is in high demand. Does not have to be a fancy certificate. You can use Udemy for example.

With this approach, you will have real testing experience, formal training, and technical skills that will make you a competitive candidate. Breaking into the industry with zero experience can take six months or more, but that time will pass anyway. Why not spend it building a solid foundation for a career that can offer growth, stability, and a chance to work in tech?

Also consider Networking:
Join QA communities, LinkedIn groups, or attend meetups to connect with professionals in the field. Networking can lead to job referrals and mentorship opportunities.

Build a portfolio to show:
Document test cases and automation scripts on platforms like GitHub. A well-organized portfolio demonstrates your technical knowledge and ability to work on real-world projects.

Get familiar with industry-standard tools like:
Automation: Playwright, Selenium, Cypress
Bug tracking: JIRA
API testing: Postman
Test management: TestRail

These tools are commonly listed as requirements in QA job postings, so knowing them will make you a more attractive candidate.

CURRENT QA TRENDS

Businesses are always looking for ways to make processes more efficient, faster, cheaper, and better whenever possible. This often leads to shifts in how testing is approached, such as transferring testing responsibilities to developers, combining roles, combining agile practices, or streamlining processes. While I welcome innovation and changes that genuinely improve efficiency, there's a fine line between being efficient and cutting corners.

The problem with cutting corners in quality processes is that it often costs far more in the long run. Software failures, service outages, crashes, and performance issues serve as reminders that quality cannot be compromised. Low quality incidents can harm user trust, damage reputations, and result in financial losses that far outweigh any initial cost savings.

Quality has been and always will be a major component of any good product or service. The challenge lies in balancing innovation with maintaining robust quality assurance practices to deliver reliable, user-friendly, and competitive products.

Some Popular Newer QA Methodologies:

There are several key methodologies that guide how QA is implemented within development workflows. These methodologies influence how, when, and by whom testing is performed.

Here's an overview of some of the most widely used QA methodologies:

- **Shift-left**

Shift-left testing means moving the testing process earlier in the software development lifecycle. Traditionally, testing happened at the end of development, but in shift-left testing, it begins at the requirement and design stages. The goal is to find and fix defects earlier, saving time and costs associated with fixing bugs later. This approach encourages collaboration between developers, testers, and product managers right from the start.

- **CI/CD (Continuous Integration Continuous Delivery)**

CI/CD focuses on automating the software development and deployment process. Continuous integration ensures that every change to the codebase is automatically tested and merged into the main branch frequently. Continuous deployment goes one step further, automatically pushing these updates to production after they pass all tests.

- **Kanban**

Kanban is a visual workflow management system that focuses on limiting work in progress (WIP) and promoting continuous flow. It uses a Kanban board with columns to track the status of each task (e.g., To Do, In Progress, In Review, Done). This system helps teams prioritize and visualize their work at every stage of the process.

- **Scrum**

Scrum is a popular agile development methodology where teams work in fixed-length periods of time called sprints (typically 1-4 weeks) to deliver product increments (new features, updates, fixes). Scrum teams hold daily stand-ups and retrospective meetings to review progress, improve processes, and address blockers. Testing is an integral part of each sprint, with testers working alongside developers to deliver quality at every stage.

- **Lean**

Lean is all about eliminating waste in processes while delivering maximum value to the customer. It focuses on reducing unnecessary steps, optimizing efficiency, and ensuring quality from the start. QA in a Lean environment is often focused on automation, continuous improvement, and just-in-time testing. Lean emphasizes speed, simplicity, and cost reduction while maintaining high-quality standards.

These methodologies are not mutually exclusive. For instance, Scrum teams often use Kanban boards, and CI/CD is a natural fit for shift-left testing. You will often see different hybrids of development approaches in real life.

The key is to combine the most effective methods to create a QA process that fits the team's needs.

BECOMING A GREAT TESTER

Becoming a great tester goes beyond simply executing test cases and finding bugs. It is about developing a mindset focused on quality, user experience, and continuous improvement. The role of a tester requires a diverse skill set that combines attention to detail, communication, problem-solving, and adaptability. Here are the core skills that define a successful QA professional:

- **Attention to detail:**

Great testers have a knack for spotting even the smallest inconsistencies, errors, or overlooked details. Whether it is a minor UI misalignment, a typo in the documentation, or a hidden edge case that could break functionality, attention to detail ensures that no defect goes unnoticed. The ability to focus on the intricacies of a product is critical because small errors often lead to significant issues down the road.

- **Strong communication skills:**

Testers act as a bridge between developers, product owners, and other stakeholders. Being able to clearly and concisely communicate findings, whether it's reporting a bug, clarifying requirements, or suggesting improvements, is essential. Effective communication ensures that issues are understood and addressed efficiently, helping the team work collaboratively toward delivering a high-quality product.

- **Understanding requirements and user needs:**

To test effectively, you need to deeply understand the product's requirements, its intended purpose, and the needs of the end-user. A good tester asks questions like, "What problem is this feature solving?" and "How would a user interact with this product?" Thinking from the perspective of the user ensures the product delivers value and meets expectations.

- **Comfort with repetitive tasks:**

While testing can involve creativity and exploration, it often includes repetitive tasks, especially when performing regression testing or executing test cases multiple times. A good tester understands the importance of consistency and accuracy, even when tasks feel monotonous. It is about staying focused on the bigger picture—ensuring quality at every stage.

- **Goal-oriented and proactive:**

A good tester is someone who keeps the end goal in mind: delivering a reliable, high-quality product. Being goal-oriented helps prioritize tasks effectively and maintain a sense of purpose. Testers also need to be proactive, anticipating potential issues and addressing them before they become significant problems.

- **Willingness to learn and adapt:**

The tech industry is constantly evolving, with new tools, methodologies, and technologies emerging all the time. A good tester is willing to learn whether it is picking up a new automation tool, understanding a new domain, or adapting to a new testing process. Continuous learning is part of the job, and staying curious ensures you remain relevant in the field.

- **Problem-solving and resourcefulness:**

Testing often involves encountering issues or situations where answers are not immediately available. A good tester knows how to figure things out—whether that means diving into the documentation, analyzing logs, experimenting with different approaches, or even Googling for answers. Resourcefulness and the ability to troubleshoot independently are invaluable traits.

- **Taking responsibility and raising the alarm:**

A tester's role is not just about finding bugs; it's about ensuring the team is aware of potential risks and problems. This sometimes means raising uncomfortable truths, such as when a feature is not ready for release or when a process needs improvement. A good tester takes responsibility for the quality of the product and is not afraid to "sound the alarm" when something needs attention. Being proactive in identifying issues shows a commitment to delivering the best possible product.

These skills are not developed overnight. They come with experience, practice, and a commitment to continuous improvement. A great tester does not just find bugs — they ensure quality is embedded in every step of the process. By mastering these core skills, you will become an essential part of any development team and a true champion of product quality.

CHAPTER 3: SDLC AND METHODOLOGIES

Navigating Testing & Quality Assurance

INTRO TO THIS CHAPTER

This section is designed for those who might be new to testing and unfamiliar with where it fits into the overall development process. Here, we will explore the basics of the Software Development Life Cycle (SDLC), common development methodologies, and how testing is integrated into these workflows.

Now, let me be clear—there are far more detailed explanations and examples available online, in other books, and even on my YouTube channel. However, my goal here is to give you a starting point.

Testing does not exist in a vacuum; it is part of a larger system that ensures the successful creation and maintenance of software. Let us dive into the basics so you can understand where testing fits and how it contributes to the bigger picture.

Again, not all methodologies are listed here. But I must tell you, one of the most important skills as a QA engineer will be the ability to do research and find information. So, start practicing that skill now and do some online research for different development methodologies popular in the tech world.

SDLC

SDLC stands for Software Development Life Cycle. It is a structured process that teams use to create software. It consists of several stages, including planning, designing, development, testing, deployment, and maintenance. The term originated around the 1960s, when computers were the size of rooms and only a handful of organizations — such as corporations, research labs, military institutions, and universities — had access to them. A step-by-step, scientific approach was required to minimize errors and maximize reliable outcomes.

Testing typically occurs after development in traditional approaches, but modern methodologies like Agile emphasize integrating testing throughout the entire cycle, with QA activities starting as early as the planning and design phases.

Each stage of the SDLC has its own goals:

- **Planning:**
  Defining the product's scope and requirements.

- **Design:**
  Outlining the architecture and user interface.

- **Development:**
  Writing the code and building the product.

- **Testing:**
  Ensuring the product meets requirements and functions as expected.

- **Deployment:**
  Releasing the product to users.

- **Maintenance:**
  Updating and fixing the product post-release.

This structured approach ensures that every stage contributes to the successful development, launch, and maintenance of a high-quality software product.

WATERFALL METHODOLOGY

Waterfall is a methodology within the Software Development Life Cycle (SDLC) that takes a linear and sequential approach to software development. It was introduced in the 1970s and mirrors the structure of the SDLC itself, moving through each phase in a step-by-step manner.

In the Waterfall methodology, each phase must be completed before moving on to the next. For example, all planning and design must be finalized before development begins, and testing only occurs after the development phase is complete.

Although Agile has gained popularity, Waterfall remains valuable in specific scenarios:

- **Highly Regulated Industries:**

In sectors like healthcare (e.g., X-rays) and aerospace, Waterfall's emphasis on documentation and process alignment ensures compliance with strict regulations.

- **Large Corporations:**

Organizations with established standards, defined budgets, and rigid timelines often find

Waterfall's structure aligns well with their needs.

- **Monolithic Products:**

For systems with clear requirements, fixed budgets, and predefined release dates, Waterfall provides predictability and control.

Waterfall thrives in environments where changes are minimal, and the project's scope is well-defined from the start.

Waterfall can struggle in dynamic environments where requirements evolve frequently. Revisiting completed phases is challenging, which can make it less flexible compared to iterative methodologies like Agile. However, when applied to the right projects, Waterfall excels at delivering high-quality, standardized products in a structured and predictable manner.

AGILE METHODOLOGY

We discussed some of the popular Agile frameworks in the Current QA Trends section, but here I wanted to provide a more general overview of what Agile is.

Agile emerged in 2001 with the creation of the Agile Manifesto, a set of guiding principles for software development. These principles emphasize flexibility, collaboration, and delivering value to customers. If you are curious,

I encourage you to search for the Agile Manifesto to explore its 12 principles, which serve as the foundation for all Agile methodologies. At its core, Agile prioritizes adaptability, the frequent delivery of working software, and a focus on individuals and interactions rather than rigid processes.

Since its inception, Agile has become the most popular methodology in software development. Its dynamic nature enables teams to adapt quickly to changing requirements and feedback, making it ideal for modern, fast-paced environments. Agile emphasizes delivering smaller, working versions of a product through iterative cycles known as sprints.

How Agile Works?

Agile thrives on collaboration. Developers, testers, and product owners work closely together throughout the development process, breaking down silos between roles. Unlike traditional methodologies like Waterfall, where testing happens only after development is complete, Agile integrates testing into every stage of the process.

Testing in Agile is continuous, ensuring that quality is maintained as the product evolves. Teams use user feedback and test results to refine and enhance the product in real-time, improving it with each sprint. This iterative approach allows teams to adapt their methods based on what works best for the project and its objectives.

Why Agile Is Effective?

- **Adapt to Change:**
Agile accommodates evolving requirements, allowing teams to
adjust without derailing progress.

- **Encourage Collaboration:**
Close collaboration across teams fosters better communication and understanding.

- **Deliver Value Faster:**
By releasing smaller, incremental updates, Agile ensures users see results sooner. Feedback from these releases can then be incorporated into the next iteration.

- **Ensure Continuous Testing:**
With testing integrated into every sprint, issues are identified and resolved early, reducing risks.

Agile is more than just a methodology; it is a mindset. It prioritizes collaboration, adaptability, and delivering value to users. By focusing on frequent delivery and embracing change, Agile empowers teams to create high-quality products that meet the evolving needs of users.

If you are new to Agile, the Agile Manifesto is an excellent starting point to understand its core values and principles.

Once you grasp these fundamentals, you will begin to see why Agile has become the dominant approach in modern software development.

Flavors of Agile

Agile is not a single methodology but a family of frameworks and practices that share the core principles of flexibility, collaboration, and delivering value. Over time, these frameworks have evolved to address the unique needs of different projects and organizations.

Some of the most common Agile methodologies include Scrum, Shift-Left, Lean, and Kanban. Each offers distinct practices while adhering to the overarching principles of Agile. Understanding these frameworks will give you a broader perspective on how Agile can be tailored to meet the needs of different teams, industries, and products.

REALITY OF METHODOLOGIES

Once you enter the job market and start working as a QA professional, you will quickly realize that the methodologies described in textbooks rarely exist in their purest form. While you may have read about Scrum, Kanban, or Waterfall as distinct and well-defined practices, the reality in most workplaces is far more fluid and hybridized.

In practice, many teams adopt a combination of methodologies, tailoring them to their specific needs and constraints. For instance, you might encounter a Kanban board for task management, but the team also holds regular Scrum meetings. Or you might find a blend of Waterfall and Agile — often humorously referred to as "Wagile" — where planning and development follow a linear process but testing and delivery incorporate iterative feedback loops.

Even within the same organization, different teams may use varying methodologies, each with its own interpretation. One team's definition of Agile might involve strict adherence to sprints and stand-ups, while another team under the same umbrella could operate more flexibly and lean toward a Kanban-style workflow.

Regardless of the methodology — or combination of methodologies — the goal remains the same: to ensure the product meets requirements, adheres to standards, and fulfills user expectations.

As a QA professional, your focus should always be on quality, no matter how the team operates.

Navigating Testing & Quality Assurance

CHAPTER 4: TYPES OF TESTING

Navigating Testing & Quality Assurance

DIFFERENT TYPES OF TESTING

Like in the previous section, I am going to introduce some of the different types of testing. However, I encourage you to do your own research and explore the various types of testing available. If you search online, you will come across dozens of testing variations, each with its own niche and purpose. In practice, though, you will likely encounter a handful of core testing types in your day-to-day work as a QA professional. Let us focus on some of the most relevant and widely used ones.

- **Regression Testing:**

Regression testing ensures that new code changes have not broken existing functionality. Whenever a new feature is added or a bug is fixed, regression testing is performed to verify that the product still works as intended. Some aspects of regression may be automated in modern QA workflows to save time and reduce repetitive manual work.

- **Exploratory Testing:**

Exploratory testing involves actively exploring the product without predefined test cases. It's about thinking like a user, asking "What if?" questions, and uncovering unexpected issues. This type of testing is especially useful for identifying edge cases and usability problems that might not be covered in formal test plans.

- **Usability Testing:**

Usability testing evaluates how user-friendly a product is. Testers observe real users interacting with the application to identify areas of confusion, inefficiency, or frustration. The goal is to ensure that the product is intuitive and easy to use.

- **Accessibility Testing:**

Accessibility testing ensures that the product is usable for people with disabilities. This might involve checking compatibility with screen readers, ensuring proper color contrast for users with visual impairments, or verifying that keyboard navigation works effectively. Accessibility is increasingly important as more organizations prioritize inclusivity and comply with regulations like WCAG (Web Content Accessibility Guidelines).

- **Feature Testing:**

Feature testing focuses on verifying that new features work as expected. This involves understanding the requirements, writing test cases, and ensuring that the feature delivers the intended functionality without introducing new bugs. Feature testing often works hand-in-hand with regression testing to maintain the product's overall stability.

- **Load Testing:**

Load testing assesses how the product performs under expected user loads. For example, how does an eCommerce site handle thousands of users browsing and purchasing items simultaneously? This type of testing identifies bottlenecks and ensures the system can handle its expected usage.

- **Stress Testing:**

Stress testing pushes the product beyond its normal operational limits to see how it behaves under extreme conditions. The goal is to identify the breaking point and ensure the system fails gracefully, without compromising user data or security.

- **Industry-Specific Testing:**

Testing practices can vary significantly depending on the industry. While the core principles of Quality Assurance remain the same—ensuring reliability, functionality, and usability—the specific requirements, methodologies, and tools often differ based on the nature of the products being tested.

For example, in healthcare, you might be testing

against standards like FHIR (Fast Healthcare Interoperability Resources) or HIPAA 5010 Healthcare EDI implementation to ensure data security and interoperability. Similarly, testing in finance might focus on regulatory compliance, while gaming might emphasize user experience and performance under high loads.

While there are many types of testing, these are some of the most common you'll likely encounter as a QA professional. As you grow in your QA career, you'll learn how to prioritize and apply these testing types effectively based on the project's needs.

CHAPTER 5: BUGS

Navigating Testing & Quality Assurance

WHAT IS A BUG?

A bug in QA (Quality Assurance) is any flaw, error, or defect in a software application that causes it to behave unexpectedly or incorrectly. Bugs prevent the software from functioning as intended, and they can impact everything from functionality to performance, usability, and security.

Bugs can occur for a variety of reasons, including human error, miscommunication in requirements, coding mistakes, or unexpected interactions between different parts of the software. Identifying and tracking bugs to resolution is a key responsibility of QA professionals, as their primary goal is to ensure the product works as expected.

One thing I want you to remember is that there is no bug-free software, but QA makes products competitive, prevents critical issues, and makes software as bug-free as possible.

While the goal of Quality Assurance is to identify and resolve defects, achieving 100% bug-free software is nearly impossible. Even products from major tech giants like Google, Microsoft, and Apple release with occasional bugs.

Here are some key reasons why perfect, bug-free software does not exist:

- **Constantly changing environment:**
Software operates in dynamic environments where devices, operating systems, and browsers are constantly being updated. A feature that works perfectly today might break after a new iOS or Android update, a browser version change, or a new hardware release.

- **Complexity of modern software:**
Modern software is built with millions of lines of code, especially in large applications like web browsers, operating systems, and enterprise tools. With so many interconnected components, dependencies, and third-party libraries, it's difficult to predict how every possible scenario will play out.

- **Limited time for testing:**
Products are often released under tight deadlines due to business pressures and market competition. Teams focus on fixing high-priority issues, but lower-priority bugs may not be resolved before release. Balancing quality and speed is a challenge, and sometimes compromises are made.

- **Infinite test scenarios:**

It's impossible to test every single user interaction. Users may click buttons in unusual sequences, enter extreme edge cases, or use the software in ways developers did not anticipate. Edge cases and unexpected user behavior often reveal hidden bugs after release.

- **Human error:**

Developers and testers are human, and humans make mistakes. Errors in logic, misinterpretation of requirements, or missed test cases can all lead to undetected bugs. Even automation scripts, which aim to catch errors, can have flaws in logic or coverage gaps.

- **Security vulnerabilities:**

Security vulnerabilities aren't always detected during testing. Hackers actively look for weaknesses that aren't apparent to the development or QA teams. Even with security testing, it's difficult to ensure every possible vulnerability is closed.

- **Miscommunication of requirements:**

Misunderstandings between business analysts, product owners, developers, and testers can lead to features being implemented incorrectly. What a developer "thinks" is correct behavior may differ from what the product owner intended. This results in a misaligned feature that may not be discovered until users report it.

- **Updates and patches:**

New features, bug fixes, and patches are released regularly. Each new release introduces the potential for new bugs due to incomplete regression testing or missed edge cases. Fixing one bug may unintentionally cause a new one.

While QA teams strive to catch as many bugs as possible, their goal is to minimize critical issues, verify product working according to requirements, reduce customer impact, and ensure product stability. **QA is a process of continuous improvement.**

BUG LIFE CYCLE

Becoming a good tester goes beyond simply executing test cases and finding bugs. Once a bug is identified, it enters the bug life cycle, a process that tracks its journey from discovery to resolution. Understanding this cycle helps ensure bugs are managed effectively and resolved in a timely manner.

1. Bug Opened:
The process begins when a tester discovers an issue and logs it in a bug tracking system.

A clear and detailed bug report should include:
- Steps to reproduce the issue.
- Expected vs. actual results.
- Supporting evidence such as screenshots or logs.
- Environment details.

After bug is opened and developer picks it up it goes to in progress.

2. In Progress:
The bug is assigned to a developer, who begins investigating and working on a fix. This stage often involves collaboration between the

developer and the tester to fully understand the issue.

3. Verified Fixed or Reopened:
Once the developer implements a fix, the tester verifies the resolution by retesting the scenario. If the issue is resolved, the bug is marked as verified fixed. If the problem persists, the bug is reopened and sent back to the developer for further action.

4. Closed:
If the fix is successful and no additional issues are identified, the bug is marked as closed, indicating it has been resolved.

This flow represents a fundamental process, but you will find variations from place to place. Always make sure to follow the framework used at your organization. Most workplaces provide examples or templates to guide you when filing a bug, so follow them closely to ensure your reports are clear and effective.

BUG TRACKING METRICS

Bug tracking metrics help QA teams measure the effectiveness of the testing process and the overall quality of the product. By tracking these metrics, teams can identify patterns, improve processes, and ultimately deliver a more stable, reliable product. Here are some key bug tracking metrics used in most QA workflows:

- **Total number of bugs:**

This is the most basic metric and tracks the total number of bugs found during testing. It gives a general sense of the application's stability. A spike in the number of bugs after a new feature is released may indicate flaws in the development process or incomplete requirements.

- **Severity and priority of bugs:**

Not all bugs are equal. Some issues are minor, while others are critical and require immediate attention. Bugs are classified by their severity (impact on functionality) and priority (urgency to resolve). Tracking these categories helps the team prioritize fixes and ensure critical issues are resolved first.

- **Bug reopen rate:**

The bug reopen rate tracks how often bugs

marked as "fixed" are later reopened due to incomplete fixes or errors in the solution.

It is calculated as:
Reopen Rate = (Number of Reopened Bugs / Total Number of Bugs) * 100

A high reopen rate may signal issues with development quality or a need for better collaboration between developers and testers.

- **Average time to resolve:**

This metric tracks the average time it takes for a developer to resolve a bug from the moment it is reported. It's useful for measuring the efficiency of the development process and identifying bottlenecks in bug resolution.

- **Escape rate (found bugs vs. escaped bugs):**

The escape rate measures the percentage of bugs that were missed during testing but found after the product was released to production.

It is calculated as:
Escape Rate = (Bugs Found in Production / Total Bugs Found) * 100

Many organizations aim to keep the escape rate between 4% to 5%, meaning 95% to 96% of bugs are caught before release.

By tracking specific bug metrics, teams can ensure better collaboration between developers and testers, optimize processes, and reduce the likelihood of issues reaching production. **Metrics like escape rate, offer valuable insights that help teams make data-driven decisions to improve product quality.**

Navigating Testing & Quality Assurance

CHAPTER 6: THE REALITY OF TESTING

Navigating Testing & Quality Assurance

INTRO TO THIS CHAPTER

Now that we've covered the core principles, let's talk about some of the pain points I've observed and experienced as a QA engineer — and more importantly, how they can be addressed. Testing is not just about following methodologies and writing test cases. It's also about navigating the challenges that arise when theory meets practice. This chapter will give you a realistic view of the QA landscape, the unexpected obstacles you may face, and strategies for overcoming them.

AUTOMATE EVERYTHING

Can we automate 100% of tests? Is a question I often hear in the software world. My take is that automation is a powerful tool that saves time, increases test coverage, and reduces repetitive manual tasks.

But in reality, automation has its limits.

In a perfect world, every aspect of testing would be automated — regression tests, performance tests, API tests, and more. But in practice, it's neither possible nor practical to automate everything. Here's why:

- **Initial investment:**
Automation requires significant time and resources to set up. Writing, maintaining, and updating scripts as the product evolves can be costly and time-consuming. Without proper planning, maintenance costs can outweigh the benefits of automation.

- **Dynamic scenarios:**
Exploratory testing relies on human intuition and creativity. Machines can follow scripts, but they can't think like users or explore unpredictable workflows. This makes it impossible to automate exploratory testing.

- **Frequent changes:**
Agile development introduces constant changes to features and interfaces. Automation scripts must be updated with every change, which can be tedious and time-consuming. Without dedicated maintenance, scripts quickly become outdated and fail.

- **Cost vs. benefit:**
Automating low-priority or rarely used features may not provide enough return on investment. Time and effort should be spent on automating critical, repetitive tasks rather than niche scenarios that may never be repeated.

Where does Automation Shine?

Despite its limitations, automation remains a crucial part of QA strategy when used correctly.

Here's where it delivers the most value:

- **Regression testing:**

Automating repetitive test cases ensures consistency and speeds up testing during frequent releases. Automation tools like Playwright, Selenium, and Cypress are commonly used for this purpose.

- **Performance testing:**

Tools like JMeter and LoadRunner can simulate thousands of users, testing system performance under heavy load — something that would be impossible to achieve manually.

- **API testing:**

Tools like Postman, REST Assured, and SoapUI help validate the behavior and reliability of backend services. Automated API testing ensures quicker feedback during development.

Automation works best for tasks that are repetitive, stable, and core to the product's functionality. Tests that involve large data sets, static outcomes, or predictable logic are excellent candidates for automation.

Finding the Balance

The key to effective testing is striking the right balance between manual and automated processes. Here's how you can achieve that:

- **Prioritize high-value automation:**

Focus on automating stable, high-priority areas of the product that are prone to repetitive testing. Target areas like login flows, data validation, and regression test suites.

- **Leverage human intuition:**

Exploratory, usability, and ad-hoc testing are best done manually, as they require human judgment, creativity, and adaptability — qualities that machines cannot replicate.

- **Continuous maintenance:**

Regularly review and update automation scripts to align with evolving product requirements. Changes in user interfaces, workflows, or third-party libraries can break scripts if they are not updated accordingly.

While automation is a powerful tool, it's not a one-size-fits-all solution. It has a specific role in a well-rounded testing strategy but must be used wisely. By understanding where automation is most effective and where manual testing is essential, you can create a balanced approach that ensures both efficiency and product quality. Automation is a tool, not the goal. The real goal is to release a stable, user-friendly, and high-quality product.

LACK OF DOCUMENTATION

One of the harsh realities of working in QA — or any role in software development — is dealing with incomplete or outdated documentation. While having clear, well-organized documentation is ideal, real-world projects rarely meet this standard.

Why Documentation Falls Short
There are several reasons why documentation is often incomplete, outdated, or missing altogether:

- **Time constraints:**

In fast-paced development environments, creating and maintaining documentation often takes a backseat to meeting tight deadlines. Teams prioritize delivering features over updating documents.

- **Evolving requirement:**

Agile workflows introduce frequent changes to features, user stories, and acceptance criteria. Documentation can quickly become obsolete, especially if no one updates it after every change.

- **Lack of ownership:**

Teams may assume that someone else (like a

product manager, business analyst, or technical writer) is responsible for updating documentation. This assumption leads to gaps, inconsistencies, or missing details.

- **Cultural neglect:**

In some organizations, documentation is simply not a priority. Teams rely on verbal communication, Slack messages, and collaboration during stand-up meetings instead of maintaining a formal knowledge base.

How This Impacts QA

For QA professionals, incomplete or outdated documentation can make testing more challenging.

Here's how it affects daily work:

- **Ambiguity:**

Without clear requirements, it's difficult to know what to test or what the expected outcomes should be. Ambiguity leads to confusion and inconsistent test coverage.

- **Wasted effort:**

When product features change but the documentation doesn't, QA testers often have to rewrite or revise test cases to match the new requirements. This can be time-consuming and inefficient.

- **Increased risk:**

The lack of documentation increases the chance that edge cases and boundary scenarios are missed. Without formal guidance, QA professionals may not know which areas of the product require extra scrutiny.

How to Navigate Documentation Challenges

While you may not have control over the state of documentation, you can take proactive steps to mitigate its impact on your QA work:

- **Ask for clear requirements:**

Don't assume things will "just fall into place." Actively seek clarification from developers, product owners, or stakeholders. If a ticket is unclear, leave comments and ask questions.

- **Participate in grooming sessions:**

Join backlog grooming, refinement, and planning sessions to stay in the loop on feature changes and requirements. This gives you a chance to ask questions in real-time and provide QA input. If something seems unclear, speak up and suggest refinement.

- **Document your insights:**
Take your own notes based on grooming sessions, developer discussions, and product demos. Use these notes as a personal reference or share them with your team. This practice can help fill in the gaps left by incomplete documentation.

- **Promote documentation culture:**
Advocate for a culture of documentation within your team. This could be as simple as encouraging your team to update JIRA tickets, add notes to Confluence pages, or provide clear acceptance criteria in user stories. Small actions like these have a cumulative impact on the entire team's efficiency.

While complete and up-to-date documentation is rare, QA professionals can bridge the gap between business, development, and documentation. By asking for clear requirements, participating in grooming sessions, and documenting your own notes, you can reduce confusion and avoid costly mistakes.

QA is not just about finding bugs or running tests; it's about connecting the dots and ensuring alignment, even when the documentation isn't perfect. Your proactive approach can make all the difference in delivering a successful product.

DEV QA

In some organizations, there's a shift toward having developers take on full responsibility for testing. In this setup, the role of QA changes from hands-on testing to more of an advisory role — guiding developers on best practices and providing feedback on their testing efforts.

While this approach may seem efficient on paper, in my opinion, it often leads to subpar testing, wasted developer resources, and higher long-term costs.

While developers are skilled at writing code, testing requires a different mindset. Testing is about finding flaws, anticipating edge cases, and thinking like a user — not just verifying that the code works as written.

Here's why relying solely on developers for testing is problematic

- **Conflict of interest:**

Developers are naturally biased toward their own work. Since they wrote the code, they tend to view it from a "this works as intended" perspective. As a result, they may unintentionally overlook defects or edge cases.

- **Lack of testing expertise:**

Testing is a specialized skill. It requires the ability to think from a user's perspective, consider unusual edge cases, and predict potential failures. Developers, while skilled in coding, may not have the necessary training or experience to design comprehensive test scenarios.

- **Reduced productivity:**

Shifting testing responsibilities onto developers takes time away from their primary role — writing and maintaining code. Instead of focusing on development, they now have to spend extra time testing, leading to slower development cycles.

- **"Work on my machine" mentality:**

Developers tend to test their code on local development environments where everything is configured to work. As a result, they focus on testing the happy path — the ideal workflow where everything works as expected — rather than testing edge cases, failure scenarios, or diverse environments.

Why This Approach Isn't Sustainable

While it may seem cost-effective to have developers handle testing, this approach is rarely sustainable.

Over time, the quality of testing declines, leading to larger issues

- **Increased bug leakage:**

More issues make it into production, frustrating users and damaging the product's reputation. Without a dedicated QA process, edge cases and defects slip through the cracks.

- **Higher long-term costs:**

Fixing bugs after release is significantly more expensive than addressing them during development. It requires emergency patches, production support, and customer service intervention — all of which increase costs.

- **Developer burnout:**

Splitting developers' focus between coding and testing can lead to burnout. Developers may feel overwhelmed with the added responsibility, reducing team morale and productivity. When burnout sets in, product quality, velocity, and developer satisfaction all decline.

What Should Developers Be Testing?

While developers should not be responsible for all testing, they should still play a role in certain types of testing.

Here's where they can focus their testing efforts:

- **Unit testing:**

Developers are best positioned to write unit tests for their own code. These tests ensure that individual functions, components, or modules behave as expected in isolation.

- **Integration testing:**

Developers should validate how their modules or components integrate with other systems, services, or APIs. Integration tests identify issues that occur when different pieces of the system interact.

- **Static code analysis:**

Developers should run static analysis tools to catch syntax errors, type mismatches, and common security flaws. This is an automated, code-level process that prevents certain issues from entering the QA pipeline.

How QA Advisers Can Be Effective

When developers are responsible for testing, QA professionals should shift their role from "test executors" to "test advisers."

Instead of running manual tests, QA should

focus on improving the quality of testing across the entire development team.

Here's how QA advisers can be effective

- **Educate developers:**
Provide training on how to write effective test cases, use testing tools, and apply the QA mindset. Teaching developers to "think like testers" will reduce the number of critical bugs that reach production. Topics like edge case identification, risk analysis, and exploratory testing should be part of this training.

- **Review developer tests:**
QA can audit and review the test cases written by developers to ensure they cover the most critical scenarios. By validating the scope and logic of these tests, QA can prevent redundant or ineffective tests while ensuring critical functionality is tested properly.

- **Lead exploratory testing:**
Facilitate exploratory testing sessions with developers, testers, and product managers. This approach promotes collaboration and allows the team to think about the product from the user's perspective. Everyone works together to discover edge cases and identify usability issues.

- **Promote automation:**
Help developers integrate automated testing into CI/CD pipelines. By adding unit, integration, and regression tests to the pipeline, the team gets immediate feedback after each build. Automation ensures that repetitive tests are executed continuously, allowing the team to focus on higher-value activities like exploratory testing.

- **Improve quality strategy:**
QA should be a driving force behind the organization's quality strategy. This includes suggesting improvements to workflows, encouraging better ticket documentation, and helping teams prioritize testing activities. QA should be the "voice of quality" in every sprint planning, grooming, and retro meeting.

Collaboration Is Better Approach

Instead of treating testing as "the developer's job" or "QA's job," a more balanced approach is collaboration.

Developers should focus on writing clean, testable code, while QA focuses on ensuring product quality through testing oversight, exploratory testing, and risk analysis.

This balance allows both developers and QA

professionals to play to their strengths:
- Developers write unit tests, integration tests, and automated tests for repetitive tasks.
- QA professionals focus on exploratory testing, edge case identification, and improving test strategy and coverage.

This collaboration leads to better products, happier teams, and fewer surprises in production. A shared responsibility for quality rather than "who owns testing" is better than just going with let developers do all the testing.

QA STRATEGY

A fundamental question every QA professional should ask is: Do we have a testing strategy? In theory, this means understanding what to test, how to test it, and which platforms or environments to support. But in reality, many organizations struggle to answer these questions, leaving QA teams without clear direction or focus.

A well-defined QA strategy provides structure and clarity, ensuring that testing efforts are aligned with business goals. It prevents teams from falling into reactive, unstructured testing and helps prioritize efforts where they matter most.

What Should a QA Strategy Include?

A comprehensive QA strategy addresses several key areas. Each of these components provides clarity on what should be tested, how testing should be done, and what risks should be accounted for.

- **Scope of Testing:**

Identify the core features, functionalities, and user flows that need to be tested. This includes focusing on critical areas like new features, high-risk areas, and frequently used functionalities.

What are we not testing?

Clearly define the out-of-scope areas to avoid wasting time on low-priority or irrelevant aspects. This prevents QA from focusing on areas that have little to no impact on the user experience.

- **Platforms and Environments:**

Establish a list of supported browsers, operating systems, and devices based on user demographics and market research. This ensures that QA efforts are directed toward environments where users are most likely to interact with the product.

Cross-browser and cross-device testing

Test the product on multiple browsers, devices, and screen resolutions to ensure consistency across environments. Cross-browser issues are one of the most common causes of production bugs.

- **Types of Testing:**

Define the required testing types, such as functional, performance, security, accessibility, and exploratory testing.

Prioritize these testing types based on the product's goals, risk level, and timeline. Some products may need intense performance testing, while others may require a stronger focus on accessibility.

- **Test Data and Scenarios:**

Plan how test data will be created, managed, and maintained. The goal is to ensure the data reflects real-world scenarios while also maintaining privacy and compliance. Use anonymized or masked production data where possible.

- **Tools and Frameworks:**

Decide which testing tools and frameworks will be used for manual and automated testing. This could include test automation frameworks like Selenium, Playwright, or Cypress, as well as bug tracking tools like JIRA.

- **Risk Management:**

Identify potential risks and areas where issues are most likely to arise. This could be high-risk modules, newly developed features, or areas of the product that frequently change.

Plan testing efforts to prioritize these risk areas, ensuring issues are caught early before they escalate.

The Reality in Most Organizations

In many organizations, these strategic decisions are either undefined or poorly communicated.

- **No clarity on scope:**
Teams are unsure which features are critical, leading to misaligned priorities. Testers may spend too much time on low-impact areas while missing the most critical workflows.

- **Undefined browser and device support:**
When there's no clear list of supported browsers and devices, QA teams may test on unnecessary platforms or miss critical compatibility issues.

- **Reactive testing:**
Without a defined strategy, testing becomes reactive. QA is often pulled into last-minute tasks or crisis testing rather than following a structured, proactive approach.

Consider this:

When QA teams don't have a clear strategy, testing efforts become scattered, inconsistent, and inefficient. Critical issues may go unnoticed until they reach production.

How to Build a QA Strategy?

If your organization lacks a formal QA strategy, you can take steps to bring structure and clarity to the testing process. Even without full control,

QA professionals can influence strategy by following these steps

- **Ask the right questions:**

Start by asking stakeholders key questions about scope, supported browsers, and risk areas. Document the answers and use them as a foundation for your testing efforts. If stakeholders can't provide answers, it signals a need for a more formal strategy.

- **Propose a plan:**

Create a draft QA strategy that outlines scope, platforms, testing types, and risk priorities. Create a high-level checklist for each module that will list what QA will cover in that module. Share this with your team for feedback and alignment. Don't wait for perfection, even a basic plan is better than none.

- **Collaborate with stakeholders:**

Work with developers, product managers, and business leaders to define testing goals and supported environments. Collaboration ensures everyone is aligned on expectations and reduces the chance of miscommunication.

- **Focus on user impact:**

Prioritize testing on areas that impact the user experience most. Test high-traffic areas, customer-facing features, and critical workflows before tackling less-used features.

What if QA has no Control?

QA is often seen as a "bug-finding" function rather than a key contributor to product quality and user experience. This narrow view reduces QA's influence on development processes.

In some companies, decisions are made by senior leadership or development teams with little input from QA. This limits QA's ability to advocate for testing best practices.

When QA operates separately from developers, product managers, and designers, it's harder to have a meaningful impact.

In fast-paced environments, tight deadlines may force teams to cut testing time. When this happens, QA is reduced to formality rather than a meaningful part of the process.

How Can QA Professionals Regain Control?

QA professionals don't need to accept a lack of control. While some factors may be out of their hands, they can take proactive steps to increase their influence:

- **Build relationships:**

Collaborate with developers, product managers, and designers. Attend planning, grooming, and design sessions to offer insights and raise potential risks early.
Be proactive

- **Don't wait to be asked:**

Propose ideas to improve processes, testing strategies, or tools. Identify gaps in the workflow and offer solutions to address them. When you spot a potential problem, be the first to raise it.

- **Communicate value:**

Share metrics that demonstrate the importance of QA, such as bugs prevented, time saved, or areas of risk mitigated.
Use clear, non-technical language to explain how QA contributes to the product's success.

- **Advocate for QA:**

Educate your team and leadership on the broader role of QA beyond just testing. Push for QA involvement in decision-making processes, such as release planning and process design.

A well-defined QA strategy provides clarity, control, and direction. Without it, teams are left reacting to last-minute changes and scrambling to test critical areas.

Even if your organization doesn't have a formal strategy, you can take the initiative. By asking the right questions, collaborating with stakeholders, and creating a plan, you can bring clarity to the testing process.

A strong QA strategy doesn't just improve testing — it strengthens the entire development process, leading to better products, happier teams, and fewer surprises in product ion.

CHAPTER 7: JOB SEARCH & CAREER GROWTH

Navigating Testing & Quality Assurance

JOIN QA COMMUNITY

Quality Assurance is a constantly evolving field, with new tools, methodologies, and industry trends emerging all the time.

To stay ahead of the curve and grow your career, it's essential to be part of a community where knowledge is shared. By connecting with others, you gain access to new perspectives, learn about best practices, and stay informed on the latest developments in QA.

- **Subscribe to QA blogs and newsletters:**
Look for industry blogs that focus on software testing, automation, and quality assurance. Popular platforms like Medium, company blogs often post useful articles. Subscribe to newsletters that summarize QA-related news, trends, and learning resources.

- **Follow QA YouTube channels:**
Many QA creators on YouTube share video tutorials, live coding sessions, and career advice. These videos can teach you about new tools, automation frameworks, and testing best practices. Consider following well-known QA creators or exploring testing content on YouTube.

- **Join online QA communities:**

Platforms like Reddit, Discord, and LinkedIn host QA-focused communities. Reddit has subreddits like r/QualityAssurance and r/softwaretesting, where you can participate in discussions, ask for advice, and get feedback on your questions.

- **Attend QA meetups and conferences:**

Look for local QA meetups or global testing conferences, either online or in-person. These events provide opportunities to network, learn from industry leaders, and discover new tools and techniques.

LEARN TRENDING TOOLS

The QA landscape is constantly evolving, with new tools and frameworks emerging to meet modern testing needs. Staying up to date with trending tools not only enhances your skill set but also makes you a more attractive candidate in the job market. Mastering modern tools allows you to work more efficiently, take on more advanced roles, and demonstrate adaptability in a field that is always changing.

- **Enroll in online courses:**

Platforms like Udemy, Coursera, and Pluralsight offer courses on popular testing tools, automation frameworks, and performance testing. Look for hands-on, project-based courses that give you practical experience

- **Get Started with Playwright:**

One of the hottest tools in QA right now is Playwright, a modern end-to-end testing framework that offers powerful automation capabilities. Many companies are adopting it as an alternative to older tools like Selenium. Learning Playwright can make you stand out as a candidate for QA roles.

- **Create GitHub Profile:**

Learning new tools is great, but showcasing your skills is even better. Building a portfolio of work that potential employers can see is one of the most effective ways to stand out in a crowded job market. A GitHub profile allows you to display your work, track your progress, and show employers that you have hands-on experience with tools like Playwright, Selenium, and Cypress.

STAY UP TO DATE

Even if you're happily employed, it's essential to keep your skills, resume, and interview readiness up to date. The QA job market evolves quickly, and new opportunities often appear when you least expect them.

Regularly updating your resume and practicing interviews ensures that you're ready to seize those opportunities when they arise.

- **Stay in touch with market demands:**

Job postings reveal what employers are currently looking for. Are more companies asking for Playwright experience? Do they expect knowledge of API testing or CI/CD tools? Monitoring job descriptions allows you to focus your learning on the most in-demand skills, ensuring you remain a competitive candidate.

- **Update Your Resume:**

Review your resume every six months and update it with new projects, skills, and tools you've used. Don't wait until you're job hunting to make these updates.

- **Update Your LinkedIn Profile:**

Keep your LinkedIn profile up to date with new accomplishments, certifications, and recent roles. This visibility increases your chances of being discovered by recruiters.

Actively connect with other QA professionals and recruiters. Engage with posts, share insights, and comment on industry-related content. This activity keeps you visible and makes it easier for hiring managers to notice you.

- **Practice Interviewing:**

Interviewing is a skill that requires consistent practice. If you only prepare for interviews once every few years, you'll feel rusty. Regularly engaging in mock interviews or real ones helps you stay confident and sharp. You'll get better at answering technical questions, discussing your experience, and navigating live coding challenges.

Staying job-ready doesn't mean you're constantly searching for a new role. It means being prepared for opportunities when they arise. By keeping your skills sharp, resume polished, and interview skills ready, you stay in control of your career, ready to make a move if the right role comes along.

Navigating Testing & Quality Assurance

CONCLUSION

If there's one key message to take away, it's this — QA is more than just "finding bugs." It's about fostering a mindset of continuous improvement, ensuring quality from the very start, and being a champion for the user experience.

Quality Assurance is a dynamic, ever-evolving field. Technology changes, tools evolve, and industry needs shift. But one thing remains constant: the need for quality.

I hope this book has provided you with practical insights, useful strategies, and a clearer understanding of the QA landscape. Finally, thank you for taking the time to read this book. Testing is a journey, not a destination. Stay curious, stay sharp, and never stop learning.

Also, check out my YouTube channel alexusadays
and my Udemy courses
https://www.udemy.com/user/aliaksandrkhvastovich/
for more insights on manual testing, Playwright automation, API testing, and many other quality assurance topics.

Wishing you success, growth, and excellence on your QA journey.

— Aliaksandr Khvastovich (aka alexusadays).